CONNOR
McDAVID

PHIL CORSO

PowerKiDS press.

New York

Published in 2019 by The Rosen Publishing Group, Inc.
29 East 21st Street, New York, NY 10010

First Edition

Editor: Elizabeth Krajnik
Book Design: Michael Flynn

Photo Credits: Cover Andre Ringuette/National Hockey League/Getty Images; pp. 4–8, 10–14, 16–23 (background) Eo naya/Shutterstock.com; p. 4 Bundit Yuwannasiri/Shutterstock.com; pp. 5, 6, 13, 17 Bruce Bennett/Getty Images Sport/Getty Images; p. 7 Ken Felepchuk/Shutterstock.com; p. 9 Chris So/Toronto Star/Getty Images; p. 11 Janet B. Kummerer/Erie Times-News/AP Photo; p. 15 Ken Andersen/Getty Images Sport/Getty Images; p. 16 Inked Pixels/Shutterstock.com; p. 18 Bill Wippert/National Hockey League/Getty Images; p. 19 Andy Devlin/National Hockey League/Getty Images; p. 20 meunierd/Shutterstock.com; p. 21 Sean M. Haffey/Getty Images Sport/Getty Images; p. 22 Harry How/Getty Images Sport/Getty Images.

Cataloging-in-Publication Data

Names: Corso, Phil.
Title: Connor McDavid / Phil Corso.
Description: New York : PowerKids Press, 2019. | Series: Young sports greats | Includes glossary and index.
Identifiers: LCCN ISBN 9781538330333 (pbk.) | ISBN 9781538330319 (library bound) | ISBN 9781538330340 (6 pack)
Subjects: LCSH: McDavid, Connor, 1997–Juvenile literature. | Hockey players–Canada–Biography–Juvenile literature. | Hockey players–United States–Biography–Juvenile literature.
Classification: LCC GV848.5.M395 C67 2019 | DDC 796.962092 B–dc23

Manufactured in the United States of America

CPSIA Compliance Information: Batch #CS18PK For Further Information contact Rosen Publishing, New York, New York at 1-800-237-9932

CONTENTS

KID BEFORE CAPTAIN

Connor McDavid may wear a captain's "C" on his jersey today, but there was once a time when he was only a little "C" skating his way up the ranks like many other hardworking young sports greats.

McDavid was born on January 13, 1997, in Richmond Hill, Ontario, Canada, and laced up his ice skates for the first time just three years later. It wasn't long into his first skate when he shook loose of his father's guiding hand and went off on his own. This was just the beginning of his life on the ice.

SPORTS CORNER

The first hockey puck ever used in an outdoor game in the 1800s was made of frozen cow poop because it was dense, or tightly packed, and smoothly moved across the ice.

SINCE HE BEGAN PLAYING HOCKEY, MCDAVID HAS PLAYED AGAINST MUCH OLDER TEAMMATES. MANY OF HIS TEAMMATES IN THE NATIONAL HOCKEY LEAGUE (NHL) ARE OLDER THAN HIM.

"BORN TO PLAY"

When McDavid was young, he watched his father Brian training with his older brother Cameron on the driveway. He wanted to train too, so he built his own **obstacle** course outside using paint cans and hockey sticks. He would practice for hours in the cold Canadian winters.

BRIAN McDAVID   CAMERON McDAVID   CONNOR McDAVID   KELLY McDAVID

MCDAVID'S PARENTS KNEW HE WASN'T LIKE OTHER YOUNG ATHLETES. WHEN HE PLAYED WITH THE OTHER KIDS, HE'D WAIT FOR THE PUCK TO COME TO HIM RATHER THAN TRY TO GET THE PUCK AWAY FROM THE GROUP OF OTHER PLAYERS.

By the time McDavid was four years old he was ready to compete. In order to play in the peewee leagues, his parents had to lie about his age, saying he was five years old. From his first game, McDavid learned just how hard he needed to train in order keep up with and outplay his older and bigger teammates and competitors.

LEARNING HOW TO WIN

McDavid was skating circles around his competition before he turned seven years old, so his parents brought him to nearby Aurora, Ontario, to play against nine-year-olds. Even then, his skills were clear to see.

From the time he was 10 years old through his early teens, McDavid played on the team his father Brian was coaching, the Aurora-based York Simcoe Express. It was on this team that he learned how to compete at a higher level. McDavid helped his team win four Ontario Minor Hockey Association titles.

These early wins pushed McDavid even further. By the time he was 14 years old, he already had **professional** hockey **scouts** checking him out.

SPORTS CORNER

If both hockey teams' goalies are injured during a game, the rules say a coach can pick anybody to play the position, including a fan from inside the arena.

MCDAVID'S SUCCESS AS A YOUNG HOCKEY PLAYER WAS ONE OF A KIND. ONE OF HIS FORMER COACHES SAID THAT HE WASN'T JUST PLAYING A GAME, BUT THAT HE WAS IN HIS OWN WORLD.

HISTORY AT 15

By 15 years old, McDavid decided to leave the York Simcoe Express and joined the AAA minor midget Toronto Marlboros of the Greater Toronto Hockey League. His skill level was beyond that of other players his age, and professional scouts were already buzzing about his future in professional hockey.

He was only the third player to ever be granted Hockey Canada's **exceptional** player status, joining John Tavares (2005) and Aaron Ekblad (2011). Reaching this level allowed him to be **drafted** a year early into the Ontario Hockey League. In his **rookie** season, he had a 15-game point streak and was named the OHL Rookie of the Month twice.

GTHL – TORONTO MARLBOROS					
YEARS	GAMES PLAYED	GOALS	ASSISTS	POINTS	PENALTY MINUTES
2011–2012	33	33	39	72	14

ON APRIL 6, 2012, MCDAVID WAS NAMED THE FIRST OVERALL PICK IN THE OHL PRIORITY SELECTION DRAFT. HE WAS PRESENTED THE JACK FERGUSON AWARD FOR BEING PICKED FIRST.

THE WORLD STAGE

After so much early success, it was time for the world to meet Connor McDavid. He stepped into the **international** spotlight in 2013 when he played in his first International Ice Hockey Federation (IIHF) World Championship **tournament** on the Canadian under-18 team in Sochi, Russia. McDavid scored the most goals, which helped Canada win its third-ever gold medal.

McDavid also played for Team Canada in the 2014 and 2015 World Junior Championships—a tournament that had become a **rite of passage** for young players looking to go pro. He captained Team North America, which won a gold medal at the 2016 World Cup of Hockey.

SPORTS CORNER

Connor McDavid chose to wear the jersey number 97 to represent his birth year, just as his favorite player Sidney Crosby of the Pittsburgh Penguins wears 87 to represent his.

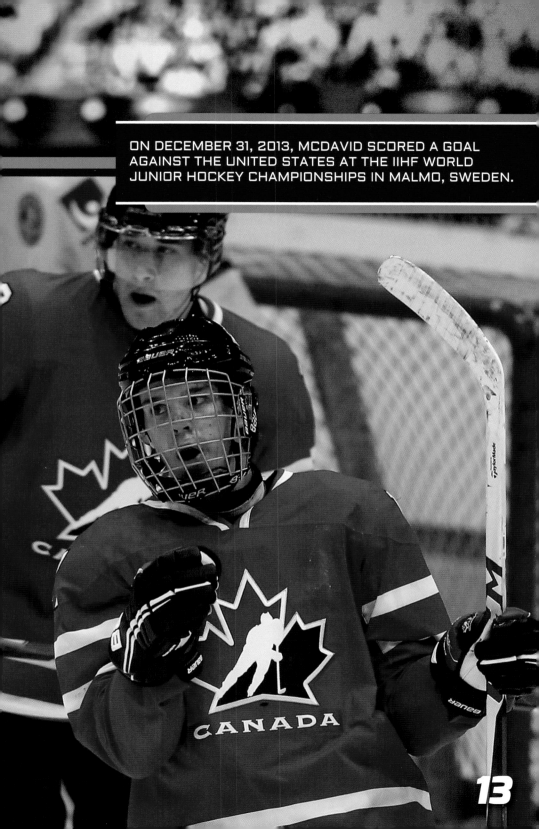

ON DECEMBER 31, 2013, MCDAVID SCORED A GOAL AGAINST THE UNITED STATES AT THE IIHF WORLD JUNIOR HOCKEY CHAMPIONSHIPS IN MALMO, SWEDEN.

NOT SO JUNIOR

McDavid didn't hold back. In his rookie season, he broke the record for most points scored by an Otters rookie with 66 points and also earned the most assists by an OHL rookie with 41.

Not long after being drafted, McDavid received a number of awards, such as the William Hanley Trophy for the OHL's Most **Sportsmanlike** Player of the Year. He was named to the 2014–2015 OHL All-Star Team.

Soon, McDavid was the most decorated player in league history. Just before the 2014–2015 season, Connor McDavid was named captain of the Erie Otters.

OHL – ERIE OTTERS					
YEARS	GAMES PLAYED	GOALS	ASSISTS	POINTS	PENALTY MINUTES
2012–2013	63	25	41	66	36
2013–2014	57	28	71	99	20
2014–2015	47	44	76	120	48

WHILE PLAYING FOR THE ERIE OTTERS, MCDAVID WAS A GREAT SCORER AND ALSO HELPED HIS TEAMMATES WITH A NUMBER OF ASSISTS.

FIRST

The 2015 NHL Entry Draft finally came on June 26, 2015. The Edmonton Oilers were lucky enough to claim that first pick and called McDavid up to the stage as the first selection of the draft.

Even though he—and the entire hockey world—knew he would be going first that night, in an interview after the draft, McDavid said he was still nervous and surprised by the feeling he got when he heard his name called. He signed a three-year entry-level contract with the Oilers just weeks later. He made the team's starting **roster** for opening night that October.

SPORTS CORNER

Connor McDavid thought about leaving the OHL to play for Boston University. Instead, he decided to continue improving his game—to the tune of 120 points in a single season.

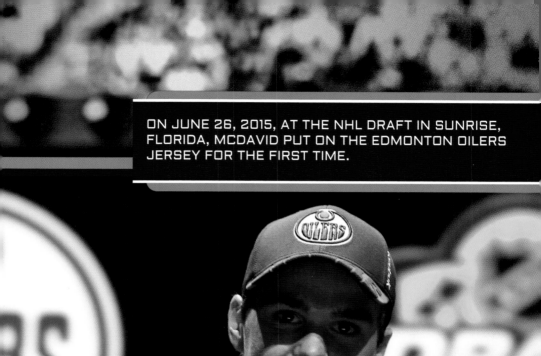
ON JUNE 26, 2015, AT THE NHL DRAFT IN SUNRISE, FLORIDA, MCDAVID PUT ON THE EDMONTON OILERS JERSEY FOR THE FIRST TIME.

NO PAIN, NO GAIN

Many people looked forward to McDavid's rookie season in the NHL. All eyes were on him to see how he would handle the change of pace from the junior league to the professional league.

However, just one month into his rookie season, McDavid broke his clavicle, or collarbone, and was sidelined for almost half of the 82-game season. It was difficult for McDavid to handle sitting out for that long.

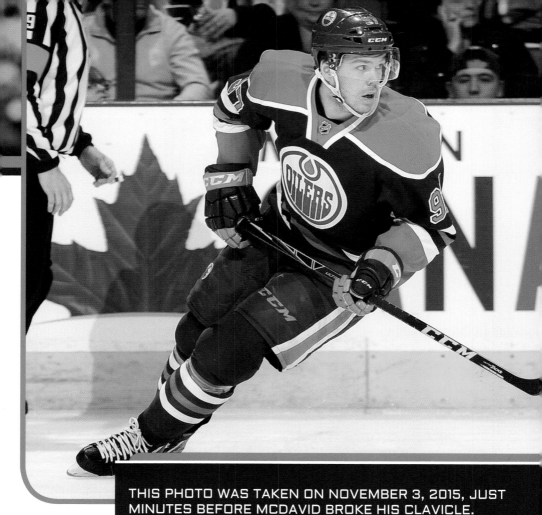

THIS PHOTO WAS TAKEN ON NOVEMBER 3, 2015, JUST MINUTES BEFORE MCDAVID BROKE HIS CLAVICLE.

He missed a total 37 games in his rookie season and learned that the higher stakes of professional hockey also meant he had to work even harder to be at the top of his game.

BOUNCING BACK

A broken clavicle could have easily broken McDavid's spirit, but he used the injury as a reason to improve his game. He returned to the ice on February 6, 2016, and scored one goal and had two assists. It was almost as if he had never been sidelined.

McDavid's bounce-back continued as he finished his rookie season with 48 points in 45 games and ranked third in the voting for the Calder Memorial Trophy given to that season's rookie of the year.

His performance led the Oilers to name him team captain the next year, making him the youngest captain in NHL history.

SPORTS CORNER

There have been misspelled words on the Stanley Cup more than 20 times in the trophy's history. They include "Bqstqn" for "Boston" and "Leaes" instead of "Leafs."

NHL – EDMONTON OILERS

YEARS	GAMES PLAYED	GOALS	ASSISTS	POINTS	PENALTY MINUTES
2015–2016	45	16	32	48	18
2016–2017	82	30	70	100	26

ON MAY 10, 2017, IN ANAHEIM, CALIFORNIA, THE OILERS PLAYED THE ANAHEIM DUCKS DURING THE 2017 NHL STANLEY CUP PLAYOFFS.

A CAPTAIN'S CONTRACT

Since his days playing peewee hockey, Connor McDavid hasn't stopped challenging himself. He signed an eight-year $100 million extension with the Oilers—the highest paid extension in NHL history. The deal is larger than the existing "big-time" contracts held by Montreal Canadiens goalie Carey Price, and Chicago Blackhawks forwards Jonathan Toews and Patrick Kane.

Looking ahead, McDavid has his sights set farther than making playoffs. As captain, he plans to help bring the Oilers to their sixth-ever Stanley Cup Championship and first since 1990, putting his name up there with former Oilers greats like Wayne Gretzky and Mark Messier.

GLOSSARY

draft: To recruit or select someone for participation with a group or organization.

exceptional: Unusually good or better than average.

international: Involving two or more countries.

obstacle: Something that makes it difficult to do something.

professional: Having to do with a job someone does for a living instead of for fun.

rite of passage: A ceremony or event marking an important stage in someone's life.

rookie: A member of an athletic team in his or her first season in that sport.

roster: A list of members of a team or organization.

scout: Someone who searches for talented young athletes in the hope of recruiting them.

sportsmanlike: Having to do with an athlete who behaves with honor and respect for the sport and its participants.

tournament: A series of contests between a number of competitors who compete for an overall prize.

INDEX

WEBSITES

Due to the changing nature of Internet links, PowerKids Press has developed an online list of websites related to the subject of this book. This site is updated regularly. Please use this link to access the list: www.powerkidslinks.com/ysg/mcdavid